Hairy Little CRITTERS

Contents

Hairy Little Critters 2
All Kinds of Hair 4
Critters with Sharp Hair 6
Hairy Swimmers 10
Hairy Tunnelers 14
Hairy Hoarders 20
Hairy Critters of the Night 22
Cleaning That Hair 26
Index 30

Hairy Little Critters

Birds have feathers and reptiles have scales, but the clever little critters in this book have coats made from all kinds of hair. They belong to a group of animals called mammals, and they live in many different habitats (or homes) all over the world. Each critter has its own strategy for survival.

All Kinds of Hair

Most mammals have hair. Fur, fuzz, whiskers, wool, and quills are all made from hair. Hair protects little critters from the weather, and its texture and color often help them blend into their surroundings, unseen by predators.

This long-nosed tree shrew blends into its Asian rain-forest home. Scientists now know that long-nosed tree shrews are related to fruit-eating monkeys. Scientists give most critters long Latin names to keep track of who is related to whom.

The furry fennec fox is the smallest fox in the world. During the day, fennec foxes sleep underground to escape the hot desert sun. Their big ears help their bodies lose heat, by acting like the radiator in a car.

The tiny elephant shrew lives in Africa. It has a special nose that looks like an elephant's trunk. It uses its nose for sniffing out bugs at night. The color and texture of its hairy coat help the elephant shrew blend into its territory.

Critters with Sharp Hair

Most mammals give birth to young that are covered with hair or fuzz. But some little critters are born with sharp hair called spines or quills. These spines and quills help provide protection against predators.

Porcupines have sharp quills. They use these quills as a first line of defense against enemies.

North American porcupines have special footpads that make them great climbers. They climb pine trees to feed on their favorite food — bark.

The spiny echidna of Australia and Papua New Guinea is a puzzling species that scientists find hard to fit into any one group of mammals. Unlike most mammals, the female echidna lays an egg in her belly pouch. Echidnas belong to a special group of egg-laying mammals called monotremes.

Hedgehogs live in Europe, Asia, southern and eastern Africa, and New Zealand. This hedgehog could have up to five thousand spines in its coat! When approached by an enemy, it will roll up into a prickly ball to protect itself. Many people like having hedgehogs in their yards. Hedgehogs prey on garden pests.

Hairy Swimmers

Most critters can swim when they have to, but some hairy little critters make a living from their amazing swimming and diving abilities. Many have special glands under their skin to make their hairy coats waterproof and warm, helping them survive in the cold waters of oceans, lakes, rivers, or streams.

Sea otters eat, play, and sleep off the coasts of Alaska and California. They are social critters, like their river otter cousins. Their thick coats have ten times as many hairs as a dog's. Oil spills, however, can destroy the waterproof quality of a sea otter's coat, causing it to freeze to death.

River otters are powerful swimmers. They swim so well that they can even outswim fish – their favorite meal. Small-clawed river otters live in Asian rain forests. Other river otter cousins live in river habitats from the Amazon to the Yukon rivers.

Muskrats aren't really rats, but like beavers, are swimming rodents. They feed on aquatic plants above and below the water's surface.

Beavers are gnawing rodents. They are the "engineers" of the animal world. With their strong jaws, they are capable of cutting down large trees for building dams and lodges in their river homes. Other animals, such as moose, benefit from the beavers' engineering projects. These animals graze the wetland habitat that forms behind the beavers' dams.

The platypus of Australia is a puzzling creature that upsets all the rules scientists use to chart the animal kingdom. Its ducklike bill and egg-laying behavior make us question if it is a bird. But platypuses are truly mammals, and nurse their young, once hatched. Platypuses are night hunters. They prey on crayfish, tadpoles, and insects. They are also diggers, making protective burrows to nest in.

Hairy Tunnelers

Some hairy little critters are tunnelers. They live in the safety of their underground homes. Sometimes a little critter will use an underground home abandoned by another animal. Many tunneling critters are hibernators. They sleep through the cold winter months.

Marmots take shelter from weather and predators by digging burrows deep into the ground.

Hoary marmots are mountainside dwellers, living high above the valley floor. Like their swimming cousins, beavers, they are members of the rodent family. Their oversized front teeth never stop growing, to make up for the wear and tear of constant gnawing.

Not all squirrels live in trees. Some species, like the golden-mantled ground squirrel, are diggers. They live in underground burrows and come to the surface to eat plants.

Prairie dogs are not really dogs. They are a species of ground squirrel. These social little critters live in underground communities called *towns*. Prairie dogs will drop into their underground homes at the first sign of danger.

Most ground squirrels are very alert. They are always on the lookout for coyotes and hawks and other enemies.

Black-footed ferrets live in prairie dog towns. Like badgers, black-footed ferrets are night hunters. Their neighbors, prairie dogs, are their favorite food! Sadly, as more and more prairie dog towns vanish, black-footed ferrets have become a very rare and endangered species.

The badger has specialized feet for digging. In North America, badgers live near prairie dog towns, where they prey on the smaller ground squirrels. Most diggers are active during the day, but badgers are night hunters.

Ermine prey on rabbits. A hungry ermine will even pursue a fleeing rabbit into its underground home.

Hairy Hoarders

Some fuzzy little critters are hoarders. They live in environments where food is scarce during the cold winter months. Hoarders store food when it is plentiful and hope they have enough to last until spring.

Pikas hoard grass and seeds. They store enough food to last through six months of snowy weather. If they fail to store enough food, they face starvation.

Beavers store branches of trees under water to eat when winter freezes the surface of their watery world.

In the autumn, squirrels hoard food for the long winter months ahead.

Hairy Critters of the Night

During the age of the dinosaurs, prehistoric hairy little critters learned that the cold-blooded dinosaurs could hunt them down in the daylight but not at night. Many mammals, with their warm coats and faster metabolisms, adapted to a nighttime life. Critters that mostly forage or hunt at night are called nocturnal, or night, critters.

Raccoons are seldom seen during the day. They are common night hunters. With their keen sense of smell, raccoons can locate birds' nests even on a dark, dark night.

Raccoons escape their predators by climbing trees.

Wetland habitats provide raccoons with lots of opportunities to catch frogs, salamanders, and fish. But they are equally at home on city streets, where they will forage for food in trash cans.

Possums, which live in New Zealand, Australia, and New Guinea, are marsupials. Female marsupials carry their young in pouches. A newborn possum is no bigger than a bumblebee and it has no fur. It will live in its mother's pouch for the first months of its life.

Possums sleep all day and emerge from their dens at night to feed.

Kit foxes are critters of the night. During the desert day, they sleep in cool underground dens. At night, they hunt for lizards and small rodents and birds. Their large, sensitive ears hear the smallest sound.

Rabbits are mostly active during the early mornings and early evenings. The activity of animals at these times is called crepuscular activity. By breaking the rules and using these in-between times of the day, rabbits can avoid day predators such as hawks, and night predators such as owls.

Cleaning That Hair

Hair traps air that helps insulate a little critter's body from the cold and the heat. But hair also traps dirt, and provides a hiding place for parasites. Many little critters spend hours keeping their coats clean.

Sea otters preen their fur constantly. Fluffed-up fur traps air bubbles that provide insulation against the cold waters.

Brushtail possums spread their toes wide to clean between each toe.

This spinifex hopping-mouse from the deserts and grasslands of Australia holds its tail still for cleaning.

The Australian sugar glider glides from tree to tree, feeding on nectar. Its sticky coat needs daily grooming.

Rabbits groom their fur regularly.

The kowari is a marsupial that inhabits the stony deserts of Australia. The female shown here is about to give birth. She is cleaning the pouch area in preparation for her newborn young.

Index

badgers 19	otters 10-11, 26
beavers 12, 21	pikas 20
black-footed ferrets 18	platypuses 13
	porcupines 6-7
echidnas......................8	possums................24, 27
elephant shrews...........5	prairie dogs 16-17
ermine........................19	rabbits 25, 28
fennec foxes.................5	raccoons 22-23
hedgehogs 9	spinifex hopping-mice 27
kit foxes 25	
kowaris 29	squirrels 16-17, 21
marmots.................14-15	sugar gliders 28
muskrats....................12	tree shrews 4

About Buck Wilde

My work as a naturalist and wildlife photographer takes me all around the world, and behind every picture there is a story.

My favorite story is about the little pika, pictured on page twenty. Annoyed by the intrusion of my camera, it charged at me and bit the soles of my heavy hiking boots.

Obviously, photographing "little critters" can be challenging – but there is always so much to learn.

WILD AND WONDERFUL
Winter Survival
Peter the Pumpkin-Eater
Because of Walter
Humphrey
Hairy Little Critters
The Story of Small Fry

ACTION AND ADVENTURE
Dinosaur Girl
Amelia Earhart
Taking to the Air
No Trouble at All!
River Runners
The Midnight Pig

FRIENDS AND FRIENDSHIP
Uncle Tease
PS I Love You, Gramps
Friendship in Action
Midnight Rescue
Nightmare
You Can Canoe!

ALL THE WORLD'S A STAGE
All the World's a Stage!
Which Way, Jack?
The Bad Luck of King Fred
Famous Animals
Puppets
The Wish Fish

Written by **Buck Wilde**
Photographed by **Buck Wilde**
Edited by **Sue Ledington**
Designed by **Kristie Rogers**
Photographic research by **Sarah Irvine**

Additional photography by **Ant Photo Library:** D. & V. Blagden (spinifex hopping-mouse, p. 27); D. Clyne (p. 29); Fredy Mercay (brushtail possum, p. 27); C. & S. Pollitt (sugar glider, p. 28); Silvestris (beaver, p. 21); **Hedgehog House:** A. & E. Bomford (young ermine, p. 19); Daniel J. Cox (p. 26); **N.Z. Picture Library:** (pp. 8-9; p. 13; p. 24; rabbit, p. 28)

© 1997 Shortland Publications Inc.
All rights reserved.

04 03 02 01 00 99
10 9 8 7 6 5 4 3 2

Distributed in the United States of America by
    Rigby
    a division of Reed Elsevier Inc.
    P.O. Box 797
    Crystal Lake, IL 60039-0797

Printed by Colorcraft, Hong Kong
ISBN: 0-7901-1670-7